God's Creative Power
for Finances

by
Charles Capps
and
Annette Capps

Unless otherwise indicated, all Scripture quotations are taken from the *King James Version* of the Bible.

Scripture quotations marked AMP are taken from *The Amplified Bible, Old Testament* copyright © 1965, 1987 by Zondervan Corporation, Grand Rapids, Michigan. *New Testament* copyright © 1954, 1958, 1987 by The Lockman Foundation, La Habra, California. Used by permission.

10 09 08   14 13 12 11 10

God's Creative Power for Finances
ISBN-13: 978-1-57794-361-7
ISBN-10: 1-57794-361-9
Copyright © 2004 by Charles Capps
P.O. Box 69
England, Arkansas 72046

Published by Capps Publishing
P.O. Box 69
England, AR 72046

Introduction

The purpose of this book, as in my previous books *God's Creative Power Will Work for You* and *God's Creative Power for Healing*, is to reveal the principles of God's Word so that you may cooperate with and apply these principles to your daily life.

The Word of God is not simply a story-book, history book, or religious book. *God's Word is creative power.* That power is still in the Word, but for it to work for you it must be released by being spoken in faith. Unfortunately, most people are speaking words of fear and failure, speaking often of the depressed economy, lack of jobs, and shortage of finances. They are saying what they have and having what they say.

I challenge you to change what you are speaking and use your words to bring God's provision into your life. By speaking and confessing these Scriptures daily, faith will be created in your heart and you will begin to see God's creative power change the circumstances of your life.

God Wants To Be Involved in Your Finances

Throughout the Bible, we see that God has a lot to say about finances. The currency of the Old Testament was silver, gold, land, crops, and herds of animals. Investments were barns filled with hay and storehouses filled with grain for sowing and feeding herds.

And Abram was very rich in cattle, in silver, and in gold.

Genesis 13:2

This was the form of currency used at the time. Today we use paper money, credit cards, and electronic banking, but the results are the same—we trade it for what we want or need.

Abraham listened to God, and God blessed and prospered him. He learned the spiritual principles of prosperity first-hand. God wanted to be involved in Abraham's finances, and He wants to be involved in yours. Let's look at some of the fundamental principles of Abraham's prosperity:

He listened to and obeyed God. (Gen. 12:1-4.)

He honored God, who prospered him. (Gen. 12:7.)

He was generous and avoided strife. (Gen. 13:5-9.)

He was compassionate toward others. (Gen. 18:24-33.)

If you want God to be involved in your finances and prosper you, you must honor these basic principles. You cannot be greedy and truly prosper. There is nothing wrong with wanting to have abundance for yourself and your family, but giving to God and being generous with others is part of the spiritual law.

There are those who [generously] scatter abroad, and yet increase more; there are those who withhold more than is fitting or what is justly due, but it results only in want. The liberal

person shall be enriched, and he who
waters shall himself be watered.

Proverbs 11:24-25 AMP

Solomon understood the principles
of prosperity. He was one of the richest
men who ever lived! His proverbs reveal
many truths regarding finances.

Honour the Lord with thy substance,
and with the firstfruits of all thine
increase: so shall thy barns be filled
with plenty, and thy presses shall burst
forth with new wine.

Proverbs 3:9-10

He who gives to the poor will not want,
but he who hides his eyes [from their
want] will have many a curse.

Proverbs 28:27 AMP

In 1 Kings chapter 3, the Lord appears
to Solomon and says, **...Ask what I shall
give thee** (v. 5). That would be a
dangerous question for some people! But
Solomon only asked for an understanding heart to help the people. God's

response was to give him wisdom, and because he wasn't greedy for himself, **I have also given you what you have not asked, both riches and honor, so that there shall not be any among the kings equal to you all your days** (1 Kings 3:13 AMP).

God wants your needs to be met abundantly! But in order to have true riches, the motive of your heart must be to bless others also and establish God's covenant.

> **And beware lest you say in your [mind and] heart, My power and the might of my hand have gotten me this wealth. But you shall [earnestly] remember the Lord your God, for it is He Who gives you power to get wealth, that He may establish His covenant which He swore to your fathers, as it is this day.**
>
> **Deuteronomy 8:17-18 AMP**

From the book of Genesis to the words of Jesus and the writings of Paul, we see proof that God does indeed want to be involved in our finances.

Wherefore, if God so clothe the grass of the field, which today is, and to morrow is cast into the oven, shall he not much more clothe you, O ye of little faith? But seek ye first the kingdom of God, and his righteousness; and all these things shall be added unto you.

Matthew 6:30,33

Beloved, I wish above all things that thou mayest prosper and be in health, even as thy soul prospereth.

3 John 2

When we get our soul to prosper and get in line with God's principles, then we can see financial prosperity manifest in our lives.

I want to share with you some of the things I have learned in my life about prosperity and finances.

My Personal Fight of Faith

Several years ago I invested quite a large sum of money in a joint business venture. I had put out a *fleece* (Judges 6:37-40) before the Lord about this business deal. Well, all the *fleeces* turned out just the way I asked. But I really got fleeced. You see, Paul said in 2 Corinthians 4:4, **In whom the god of this world hath blinded the minds of them which believe not, lest the light of the glorious gospel of Christ, who is the image of God, should shine unto them.** Paul said satan is the god of this physical world, and satan knew the fleece I had put out.

Now I have found a better way to find the will of God. **Howbeit when he, the *Spirit of truth,* is come, *he will guide you into all truth:* for he shall not speak of himself; but whatsoever he shall hear, that shall he speak: and he will shew you things to come** (John 16:13).

I had sold a small farm and invested the money in this business. I lost nearly all the original investment plus $25,000 more.

Through the confusion the enemy caused, I *lost faith* and *turned negative on life.* I thought God had done this to me. That was what satan had put in my mind. After several months, I realized that the *negative thoughts* in my mind did not agree with the *Word of God.*

Then the enemy tried to convince me that I had failed God and He was mad at me and that was the reason I had lost the money.

I know this story sounds familiar to many because it is one of satan's favorite lies that he uses to bring condemnation and confusion to God's people.

My Confessions Ruled

In that confused state of mind, I turned negative. I began to say, "It doesn't matter what I do—it won't work out anyway."

I was still farming about 800 acres of land at that time, so I turned my attention to the farming operation. I knew that was one thing I could do well because I had always been successful in it.

But after I had *turned negative*, I would plant cotton and say, "Well, it doesn't make any difference how deep I plant it; it will probably rain three inches and it won't come up anyway."

It did rain, and the cotton didn't come up.

I planted again, this time shallow—about one-half inch deep—and told almost everyone I saw, "Now it will turn off dry and won't rain for three weeks."

And it did just what I said.

The third time I planted that year, I made *more negative statements*. The more problems showed up, the more negative I became (this is satan's cycle). The third planting produced about two-thirds of a stand of cotton. I can, even now, still hear my words: "Now there will probably come an early freeze and kill it before it opens."

And it did.

For two whole years I confessed the same thing and got just what I said. I farmed 800 acres those two years and did not make enough money to buy my driver's license. The farming practices that once worked for me did not work. The same ground that once produced bountifully now refused to respond.

I was still giving. I still believed Luke 6:38, **Give, and it shall be given unto you; good measure, pressed down, and shaken together, and running over, shall men give into your bosom. For with the same measure that ye mete withal it shall be measured to you again.** But it was not working for me. I prayed, I repented, I begged God to prosper me—but nothing worked. I was still negative. My confession destroyed my prayer. I saw failure everywhere I looked. I believed it and confessed it daily. I was a failure. I was at the end of my rope financially. I had just borrowed $100,000 to pay my back bills. I was so poor I couldn't pay attention. I would go to church, but I couldn't get anything out of the service because I was worrying about my finances.

Then, a Baptist man came to my house one day. He had some books with him. I remember thumbing through one of the books and reading a few paragraphs here and there. The title of the book was *Right and Wrong Thinking*, by Kenneth Hagin. It was different from any book I had ever read. Every paragraph said something, and it was straight to the point. I remember to this day one of the first statements I read: *"People that think wrong believe wrong, and when they believe wrong, they act wrong."*[1]

It went off inside me like a bombshell. It just seemed like someone turned a light on inside me. **The entrance of thy words giveth light; it giveth understanding unto the simple** (Ps. 119:130). I knew instantly that this was truth.

I ordered that book and another one on confessions. I began to *dig* into the Word of God to see where I was missing

---

[1] Kenneth E. Hagin, *Right and Wrong Thinking*, (Broken Arrow, Oklahoma: Kenneth Hagin Ministries, 2nd Edition, 1986).

it. I had never heard anyone preach on Mark 11:23-24, **For verily I say unto you, That whosoever shall say unto this mountain, Be thou removed, and be thou cast into the sea; and shall not doubt in his heart, but shall believe that those things which he saith shall come to pass; he shall have whatsoever he saith. Therefore I say unto you, What things soever ye desire, when ye pray, believe that ye receive them, and ye shall have them.**

I am sure I had read it, but it meant nothing to me. It was not in me. I had no idea you could have what you say. But as I began to *prayerfully study* what Jesus said about *WORDS,* the mouth, and prayer, God began to reveal these things to me.

I remember one morning I was praying, and I said, "Father, I have prayed and *it is not working out.*"

He spoke inside my spirit plainly, "What are you doing?"

I said, "I am praying."

15

He said, "No, you're not. You are complaining." Then He said, "Who told you it is not working out?"

Now that shook me. I thought for a minute, and then I said, "Well, I guess the devil said that."

Then He spoke into my spirit some things that totally transformed my life. He said, "I would appreciate it if you would quit telling me what the devil said. You have been praying for me to prosper you and get the devil off of you. I am not the one that is causing your problems. You are under an attack of the evil one, and I can't do anything about it. You have bound Me by the words of your own mouth. And it is not going to get any better until you change your confessions and begin to agree with My Word. You are operating in fear and unbelief. You have established the words of the evil one in your behalf. By your own mouth you have released the ability of the enemy. If I were to do anything about it, I would have to violate My Word—and I can't do that."

I had just gotten enough of His Word in me that He could talk to me intelligently about the problem. Until then, He had no basis on which to talk to me, for I had cast out His Word and quoted the enemy. Over a period of the next few months, He spoke many things into my spirit that totally *upended my way of thinking*.

He said, "I am for you; I want you to prosper, but I want you to do it in a way that will work an eternal value in you, by using your faith and acting on the Word. The power of binding and loosing is not in heaven. It is on earth, and if you don't do it, it won't be done." Then He told me this: "Study and search My Word for promises that pertain to you as a believer. Make a list of these, and confess them aloud daily. They will build up your spirit over a period of time. Then, when these truths are established in your spirit, they will become true in you."

You Can Have What You Say

Most Christians who are defeated in their finances are defeated because they believe and confess the wrong things. They have spoken the words of the enemy, and those words hold them in bondage. Jesus said in Matthew 17:20, **...for verily I say unto you, If ye have faith as a grain of mustard seed, ye shall say unto this mountain, Remove hence to yonder place; and it shall remove; and nothing shall be impossible unto you.**

And in Mark 11:23, **For verily I say unto you, That whosoever shall say unto this mountain, Be thou removed, and be thou cast into the sea; and shall not doubt in his heart, but shall believe that those things which he saith shall come to pass; he shall have whatsoever he saith.**

In these passages of Scripture, Jesus tells us that what we believe and speak affects the natural world, including our finances. God has given us His Word so that we can understand these spiritual laws that govern the universe. There are spiritual laws just as there are natural laws, such as gravity and the law of lift. When you work *with* these laws, they work for you. When you work against God's spiritual laws, they work against you.

When you speak negatively about your financial situation, you can have what you say and believe.

Here is a very important spiritual law: *You can have what you say.*

With your words you can choose life or death, poverty or riches, sickness or health. You may tithe (give 10 percent to the church), work hard, and pray for prosperity every day, but if your words are negative and contrary to God's Word, you could stay mired in debt, struggling to make ends meet.

Words are powerful, but God's Word is full of creative power. When you agree with what God has said about you and speak His Word, your circumstances will begin to change and line up with His will for your life.

God's Will Is for You To Prosper

Beloved, I wish above all things that thou mayest prosper and be in health, even as thy soul prospereth.

3 John 2

If you have any doubt that God wants you to prosper, you will not be able to release faith for your finances. Whatever you believe and speak will control your financial situation. Begin by confessing what God's Word says about your finances:

God's will is for me to prosper and be in health as my soul prospers. (3 John 2.)

The Lord has pleasure in the prosperity of His servant, and Abraham's blessings are mine. (Gal. 3:14; Ps. 35:7.)

As you confess what God says about you, it changes you and your circumstances. If you have any doubt about God's will for your prosperity, read Deuteronomy chapter 28. God told

Moses and the children of Israel that blessing and cursing were before them. If they chose to **hearken diligently unto the voice of the Lord** and do all His commandments, then they would be blessed in every area. (v. 1.) Everything they touched would prosper.

If they chose to **not hearken unto the voice of the Lord,** then they would be cursed with poverty, sickness, and spiritual death. (v. 15.)

Poverty is a curse just as surely as sickness and spiritual death are curses. But Christ has redeemed us from the curse of the law!

> **Christ hath redeemed us from the curse of the law, being made a curse for us: for it is written, Cursed is every one that hangeth on a tree: that the blessing of Abraham might come on the Gentiles through Jesus Christ; that we might receive the promise of the Spirit through faith.**
>
> **Galatians 3:13-14**

One of the curses in Deuteronomy 28 was the curse of poverty and financial destruction. We have been redeemed from financial destruction! Declare your financial redemption! God already has!

The blessing of Abraham included financial prosperity. He became a very rich man. Through Jesus, the blessings of Abraham have come upon us as we receive the promise through faith in God's Word!

Too many Christians think that prosperity is a curse. But that is not true—they have been deceived. I talked with a Christian lady who in conversation remarked, "I'm just poor and I can't afford the things other people can buy." That may have been a true statement of her current financial status, but what amazed me was that she said it with pride and a sense of self-righteousness. It was obvious that she thought she was a better Christian because she was poor.

God's Word states that poverty is a curse. Just look at God's real intent:

> **But thou shalt remember the Lord thy God: for it is he that giveth thee power to get wealth, that he may establish his covenant which he sware unto thy fathers, as it is this day.**
>
> **Deuteronomy 8:18**

If you can be convinced that poverty is a blessing, then God will not be able to establish His covenant *through you.* If you live in poverty and financial lack, these words are not a judgment against you. You may be poor, but don't be proud of it! To get out of poverty, you have to let go of it and whatever advantage you think it provides for you.

Change What You Say

Don't let your words of doom and failure defeat you in life. Set a watch on your mouth and stop those doubt-filled, negative words. They do not agree with God.

When things look bad, it's better to keep your mouth shut than to go around "poor-mouthing," telling everyone your financial woes. You'll dig yourself a hole so deep that you may never get out! But if you take time to program your heart by saying what God says about you, you can have victory over apparent financial defeat.

> **Jesus answered and said unto them, Verily I say unto you, If ye have faith, and doubt not, ye shall not only do this which is done to the fig tree, but also if ye shall say unto this mountain, Be thou removed, and be thou cast into the sea; it shall be done.**
>
> **Matthew 21:21**

> **...but shall believe that those things which he saith shall come to pass; he shall have whatsoever he saith.**
>
> **Mark 11:23**

Think about it: Do you really want everything you say to come to pass? This is spiritual law. If you speak God's Word after Him until you believe and doubt not in your heart, then Jesus said you will have what you say.

Strike these popular phrases from your vocabulary:

"Money doesn't grow on trees."

"I can't afford...."

"I am on a fixed income."

Statements such as these put you in bondage to a belief in lack and hold your finances in bondage.

Plant Seed for Your Prosperity

When you speak God's Word over your finances, you are planting seeds that will grow and produce abundantly for you. In Mark chapter 4, Jesus gives us the Parable of the Sower. In verse 14, He immediately tells us what is being sown: **The sower soweth the *word*.**

If you sow the seed of God's Word in the good ground of your heart by speaking it, it will produce in your life.

And these are they which are sown on good ground; such as hear the word

**and receive it, and bring forth fruit,
some thirtyfold, some sixty, and some
an hundred.**

Mark 4:20

Whatever you sow, you will reap. This, too, is spiritual law. When you sow words of doubt and fear over your finances, you will get exactly what you fear: lack! Don't allow your words to defeat you! Life and death are in the power of your tongue. Plant a crop for what you want, not what you don't want.

Jesus said in Luke 6:38, **Give, and it shall be given unto you; good measure, pressed down, and shaken together, and running over, shall men give into your bosom.**

To reap financial blessing, you sow seeds by giving. Sow in faith for the finances that you need. It takes a seed to produce a harvest. A seed could be whatever you have. If you only have one dollar, then sow that seed. It could yield a hundred-fold crop. If you don't have one dollar, then give away something you possess. Give it with the intent to help someone in need, as well as sowing a seed for your financial prosperity.

Malachi 3:10 says, **Bring ye all the tithes into the storehouse, that there may be meat in mine house, and prove me now herewith, saith the Lord of hosts, if I will not open you the windows of heaven, and pour you out a blessing, that there shall not be room enough to receive it.**

Your tithing and giving create a financial relationship with God and His Word, which makes the possibilities unlimited. Jesus said, **...all things are possible to him that believeth** (Mark 9:23).

Speak to Your Mountain

Several years ago, I started a housing subdivision north of the town of England, Arkansas. I had borrowed money to put in water, sewer, and streets, and I had a mountain of debt. Jesus said to speak to the mountain and it would be removed. I

27

got all the mortgages out and laid them on the kitchen table. I called my daughter Annette and said, "I want you to be a witness that I'm going to do what Jesus said to do." I said: "Notes, listen to me, I'm talking to you. Jesus said you would obey me. In the name of the Lord Jesus Christ, I command you, I say to you, BE PAID IN FULL...DEMATERIALIZE...DEPART...BE GONE.... IN JESUS' NAME, YOU WILL OBEY ME!"

I turned around and walked off and left my daughter standing there. She had seen me do some strange things before. Someone asked, "Didn't you feel a little silly doing that?" No. I felt a lot silly! But feelings have nothing to do with it. Jesus said to speak to the mountain, speak to the sycamine tree, and it would obey you. So many people tend to spiritualize the Word of God, but it is very practical.

I had two houses in this subdivision that I had built to sell. I had prayed and asked God to send a buyer, but the houses hadn't sold. One day as I drove out there, I asked, "Lord, why haven't these houses sold?" He spoke into my spirit, "Because you didn't do what I said to do. Do what you have been teaching other people to do." I got out of my truck and said, "Houses, now listen to me. I'm talking to you. Someone's impressed with you and you will be a blessing to someone. I call you SOLD in Jesus' name!"

The houses didn't sell overnight, and my carnal mind said, "Now what are you going to do?" I said to myself, "I know what I am going to do. I'll release my faith in laughter." I drove over to one house, rolled down the window, looked both ways down the street and said, "Ha ha ha." I drove in front of the other one and said, "Ha ha ha," rolled up the window and drove home.

You have to learn to laugh at your problems. Tears of self-pity and sorrow never release faith. I simply did what the Spirit of God told me to do.

Over the next few months, not only did the houses sell, but I sold the entire subdivision and all the land behind the subdivision that was not developed. The notes and mortgages were paid in full!

Take Authority Over Your Finances

If you are in debt, then you can exercise your authority as a child of God and call your debts paid. Jesus said, **If you had faith (trust and confidence in God) even [so small] like a grain of mustard seed, you could say to this mulberry tree, Be pulled up by the roots, and be planted in the sea, and it *would obey you*** (Luke 17:6 AMP). Think about it: paper money, notes, and mortgages are made out of trees and Jesus said the tree *would* obey your faith filled words. Philippians 2:9 says that God has highly exalted Jesus and given Him a name above every name. Verse 10 says, **That at the name of Jesus every knee should bow, of things in heaven, and things in earth, and things under the earth.**

Jesus has given us the right to use His name. Speak to your finances and tell them to come in line with God's Word. The declarations listed below will enable you to take authority over financial issues by putting the creative power of God's Word in your heart and in your mouth. You, too, can speak to the mountain and see it removed!

DECLARATIONS*

*To be spoken boldly and authoritatively with emphasis on capitalized words.

To Eliminate Debt

Take copies of mortgages, notes, credit card debt, past due bills, delinquent taxes, and other papers representing your debt, and lay them out before you. Boldly declare on the authority of God's Word:

> *In Jesus' name and on the authority of His Holy Word, I call these debts PAID IN FULL! Debt, I speak to you in Jesus' name: BE PAID and BE GONE! Dematerialize and CEASE TO EXIST! I now declare that all my debts, mortgages,*

and notes are PAID IN FULL, *CANCELLED, or DISSOLVED!*

To Collect Money Owed to You, or Accounts Receivable

If there are people who owe you money or clients who owe your business money, you can loose those finances to flow to you. Make a list of those people, businesses, or organizations. Place the list in front of you, lay your hands upon it, and declare:

Jesus said whatever I loose on earth is loosed in heaven; therefore, I LOOSE *the finances that are owed to me. I call this money in so that these accounts are* PAID *in Jesus' name!* (Matt. 18:18.)

Timely Payment of Monthly Bills

Put your bills in a stack. Lay your hands upon them, and declare out loud:

God supplies all my needs according to His riches in glory

by Christ Jesus. God is the source of my supply, and I have more than enough to pay my bills on time. BE PAID IN FULL!
(Phil. 4:19.)

To Sell Property

Make certain that the price you are asking is a fair exchange. Proverbs 20:23 says that deceitful weights (used to measure worth) and false scales are shamefully vile to God. You can talk to your property and say to it:

Listen to me. I am talking to you. Jesus said you would obey me. You are going to be a blessing to someone and I call you SOLD IN JESUS' NAME!

To Buy Property

I call those things that be not as though they were. I now call the property that fits my needs and desires and will be a blessing to me. I CALL YOU TO ME NOW IN JESUS' NAME! I declare that God's highest and best is done in this matter and the angels are now working on my behalf. (Rom. 4:17.)

To Remove Hindrances

God, Your Word says that whatever I bind on earth is bound in heaven and whatever I loose on earth is loosed in heaven. Therefore, on the authority of Your Word, I bind every force that has set itself against my financial prosperity! I HEREBY DECLARE ALL CURSES AGAINST ME NULL, VOID, AND HARMLESS! I AM REDEEMED FROM THE CURSE OF POVERTY! I AM FREE FROM OPPRESSION! I now loose the abundance of God, and all that rightfully belongs to me now comes to me under grace in a perfect way.

Calling Things That Are Not
To Increase Your Paycheck

As an employee, you act in faith by performing your job with the highest integrity and diligence. Act as if you are a highly paid employee. If possible, tithe in faith in advance for your raise or promotion. Hold your paycheck or stub in your hand, and say:

> *Heavenly Father, I call for a raise as I honor You with the firstfruits of my increase. I give thanks for this job and bless my employer. I now declare that this check is multiplied and increased. I am now richly rewarded for my work, both creatively and financially.* (Prov. 3:9-10.)

To Increase Your Investments and Bank Accounts

Make a list of your investments and bank accounts, or use bank statements. Place them in front of you and proclaim:

I call for abundance as I honor the Lord with my capital and sufficiency. My storage places (investments and bank accounts) are filled with plenty, and my presses burst forth with new wine. I am abundantly supplied. (Prov. 3:9-10 AMP.)

For Employment

I now dissolve and put aside all negative, limiting beliefs about where I will work and what kind of job is available to me. I open myself to all of God's possibilities. I call for a perfect, satisfying, well-paying job to manifest in my life. I am always in the right place at the right time, for the Spirit of God directs my steps. (Prov. 16:9; Rom. 5:17.)

Watch Your Words

It is vital that you speak only the end result and what you desire. Don't counteract the declarations you have spoken in faith. Manifestations may not come immediately. Hold fast to your confession. Do not speak contrary or foolish words. Say what you mean, and mean what you say. Speak as if every word you say will come to pass. You can fill your heart and mouth with faith by daily voicing scriptural confessions. (Heb. 10:23; Rom. 10:8.)

Program Your Spirit for Success

Make these confessions daily until faith comes.

I am filled with the knowledge of God's will in all wisdom and spiritual understanding. His will is my prosperity. (Col. 1:19.)

* * *

God delights in my prosperity. He gives me power to get wealth, that He may

establish His covenant upon the earth.
(Deut. 8:18; 11:12.)

* * *

I immediately respond in faith to the guidance of the Holy Spirit within me. I am always in the right place at the right time because my steps are ordered of the Lord. (Ps. 37:23.)

* * *

God has given me all things that pertain to life and godliness, and I am well able to possess all that God has provided for me. (Num. 13:30; 2 Peter 1:3-4.)

* * *

God is the unfailing, unlimited source of my supply. My financial income now increases as the blessings of the Lord overtake me. (Deut. 28:2.)

* * *

As I give, it is given unto me, good measure, pressed down, shaken together, and running over. (Luke 6:38.)

* * *

I honor the Lord with my substance and the firstfruits of my increase. My barns are filled with plenty, and my presses burst forth with new wine. (Prov. 3:9-10.)

* * *

I am like a tree planted by rivers of water. I bring forth fruit in my season, my leaf shall not wither, and whatever I do will prosper. The grace of God even makes my mistakes to prosper. (Ps. 1:3.)

* * *

I am blessed in the city, blessed in the field, blessed coming in, and blessed going out. I am blessed in the basket and blessed in the store. My bank accounts, investments, health, and relationships flourish. The blessings of the Lord overtake me in all areas of my life. (Deut. 28:1-14.)

* * *

The blessing of the Lord makes truly rich, and He adds no sorrow with it. (Prov. 10:22.)

* * *

My God makes all grace abound toward me in every favor and earthly blessing, so that I have all sufficiency for all things and abound to every good work. (2 Cor. 9:8.)

* * *

The Lord has opened unto me His good treasure and blessed the work of my hands. He has commanded the blessing upon me in my storehouse and all that I undertake. (Deut. 28:8,12.)

* * *

I delight myself in the Lord, and He gives me the desires of my heart. (Ps. 37:4.)

* * *

The Lord rebukes the devourer for my sake, and no weapon that is formed against my finances will prosper. All obstacles and hindrances to my financial prosperity are now dissolved. (Mal. 3:10-11; Isa. 54:17.)

* * *

My mind is renewed by the Word of God; therefore, I forbid thoughts of failure and defeat to inhabit my mind. (Eph. 4:23.)

* * *

I am delivered from the power and authority of darkness. I cast down reasonings and imaginations that exalt themselves against the knowledge of God, and I bring every thought into captivity to the obedience of God's Word. (2 Cor. 10:3-5.)

* * *

I am filled with the wisdom of God, and I am led to make wise and prosperous financial decisions. The Spirit of God guides me into all truth regarding my financial affairs. (John 16:13.)

* * *

The Lord causes my thoughts to become agreeable to His will, and so my plans are established and succeed. (Prov. 16:3 AMP.)

* * *

There is no lack, for my God supplies all my needs according to His riches in glory by Christ Jesus. (Phil. 4:19.)

* * *

The Lord is my shepherd, and I do not want. Jesus came that I might have life and have it more abundantly. (Ps. 23:1; John 10:10.)

* * *

Having received the abundance of grace and gift of righteousness, I reign as a king in life by Jesus Christ. (Rom. 5:17.)

* * *

The Lord has pleasure in the prosperity of His servant, and Abraham's blessings are mine. (Ps. 35:27; Gal. 3:14.)

* * *

Angels Are Listening

God's throne is established in heaven and His kingdom rules over all. (Ps. 103:19.) The angels were created as ministering spirits to minister for those who are heirs of salvation. (Heb. 1:14.) One of the ways they minister to and for us is by taking heed to our words when we are speaking God's Words after Him. If we are giving voice to God's Words of promise, then angels have an assignment to see to it that that promise is eventually fulfilled in your life. They know Jesus said you can have what you say if you believe and doubt not. They are to do God's pleasure (v 21), and God has pleasure in the prosperity of His servants.

You Have Supernatural Help

When we give voice to God's Word on a daily basis, the angels and the Holy Spirit work diligently in arranging our prosperity. They see to it that we are led by our spirits to be in the right place at the right time so that we will have the promises of God that we are confessing to be manifest in our lives. Always remember that God has pleasure in the prosperity of His servants and Abraham's blessings are yours because of the abundance of grace manifest to us through Jesus Christ our Lord.

As you make these daily confessions, you may feel as if they are not true, but faith comes by hearing the Word of God, hearing yourself saying what God said about you. (Rom. 10:17.) Faith will come, and one day you will wake up and feel rich even though you may not have a dollar in your pocket. Your feelings will fall in line with the Word of God.

God created the universe by the methods which you have just put into motion: by the power of His Words. Man is created in the image of God and releases his faith in words. The Word of God, conceived in the human spirit, formed by the tongue, and spoken out of the mouth, is creative power that will work for you.

Prayer of Salvation

God loves you—no matter who you are, no matter what your past. God loves you so much that He gave His one and only begotten Son for you. The Bible tells us that **...whoever believes in him shall not perish but have eternal life** (John 3:16 NIV). Jesus laid down His life and rose again so that we could spend eternity with Him in heaven and experience His absolute best on earth. If you would like to receive Jesus into your life, pray the following prayer out loud and mean it from your heart.

Heavenly Father, I come to You admitting that I am a sinner. Right now, I choose to turn away from sin, and I ask You to cleanse me of all unrighteousness. I believe that Your Son, Jesus, died on the cross to take away my sins. I also believe that He rose again from the dead so that I might be forgiven of my sins and made righteous through faith in Him. I call upon the name of Jesus Christ and confess Him to be the Savior and Lord of my life. Jesus, I choose to follow You and ask that You fill me with the power of the Holy Spirit. I declare that right now I am a child of God. I am free from sin and full of the righteousness of God. I am saved in Jesus' name. Amen.

About the Authors

Charles Capps is a retired farmer, land developer, and ordained minister who travels throughout the United States sharing the truth of God's Word. He has taught Bible seminars for thirty years, sharing how Christians can apply the Word  to the circumstances of life and live victoriously.

Besides authoring several books, including the bestselling *The Tongue—A Creative Force*, and the minibook *God's Creative Power*, which has sold over 4 million copies, Charles Capps Ministries has a national daily syndicated radio broadcast and a weekly television broadcast aired over several networks called "Concepts of Faith."

For a complete list of CDs, DVDs, and books by Charles Capps, or to receive his publication, *Concepts of Faith*, write:

Charles Capps Ministries
P.O. Box 69
England, Arkansas 72046

Or visit him on the Web at:
www.charlescapps.com

Annette Capps is the daughter of author and teacher Charles Capps. She is an ordained minister, businesswoman, and pilot. Since the age of 14, she has ministered in churches and several foreign countries. A licensed pilot, she  has flown her airplane throughout the United States, conducting seminars on a wide range of Bible subjects.

In addition to the book, *Quantum Faith*, Annette has authored two other books entitled, *Reverse the Curse in Your Body and Emotions* and *Understanding Persecution*.

For a complete list of CDs, DVDs, and books by Annette Capps, write:

Annette Capps Ministries
P.O. Box 69
England, Arkansas 72046

Or visit her on the Web at:
www.annettecapps.com
1-877-396-9400

Books by Charles Capps

Jesus, Our Intercessor
Hope—A Partner to Faith
Seedtime and Harvest
Success Motivation Through the Word
The Tongue—A Creative Force
Releasing the Ability of God Through Prayer
God's Creative Power Will Work for You
Authority in Three Worlds
Angels
Faith and Confession
God's Creative Power for Healing

Books by Annette Capps

Understanding Persecution
Reverse the Curse
Quantum Faith